BULLYING with
TEASING, NAME-CALLING, AND RUMORS

Addy Ferguson

PowerKiDS press.

New York

Published in 2013 by The Rosen Publishing Group, Inc.
29 East 21st Street, New York, NY 10010

First Edition

Editor: Jennifer Way
Book Design: Erica Clendening and Colleen Bialecki

Photo Credits: Cover Paul Viant/The Image Bank/Getty Images; pp. 4–5, 9, 12, 17, 18 iStockphoto/Thinkstock; p. 6 Pixland/Thinkstock; p. 8 Baerbel Schmidt/Stone/Getty Images; p. 10 BananaStock/Thinkstock; p. 11 Elena Elisseeva/Shutterstock.com; p. 13 © iStockphoto.com/Christopher Futcher; p. 14 Fuse/Getty Images; p. 16 JupiterImages/Brand X Pictures/Thinkstock; p. 19 Creatas/Thinkstock; p. 20 Comstock/Thinkstock; p. 21 Design Pics/Thinkstock; p. 22 Digital Vision/Thinkstock.

Library of Congress Cataloging-in-Publication Data

Ferguson, Addy.
  Bullying with words : teasing, name-calling, and rumors / by Addy Ferguson. — 1st ed.
      p. cm. — (Stand up: bullying prevention)
  Includes index.
  ISBN 978-1-4488-9670-7 (library binding) — ISBN 978-1-4488-9798-8 (pbk.) —
  ISBN 978-1-4488-9799-5 (6-pack)
  1. Bullying—Juvenile literature. 2. Teasing—Juvenile literature. 3. Verbal behavior—Juvenile literature.
  4. Aggressiveness in children—Juvenile literature. I. Title.
  BF637.B85F4674 2013
  302.34'3—dc23
                                          2012027305

Manufactured in the United States of America

CPSIA Compliance Information: Batch #W13PK4: For Further Information contact Rosen Publishing, New York, New York at 1-800-237-9932

Contents

What Is Bullying?

Bullies look for people they think are weaker or different, and they target them. They hurt, scare, threaten, **humiliate**, or **exclude** their target.

A verbal bully might not hit his victim, but the cruel names and taunts he uses are hurtful.

Cyberbullies also use words to hurt or threaten others. They might even find it easier than other bullies to hurt other people because they do not have to do it face-to-face.

Physical bullies use their bodies to bully. They push, shove, hit, or otherwise hurt their victims. **Cyberbullies** use texting, e-mails, social-networking sites, and other online tools to spread rumors and lies. There are also social bullies, who get other people to exclude a target. **Verbal** bullies are those who use words to hurt. As you can see, there are many ways bullies can hurt others.

Bullying with Words

Let's look closely at verbal bullying. Verbal bullies call their targets names, taunt and embarrass them, and may spread false rumors about them.

Unlike friends who tease each other, the words of verbal bullies are not spoken in fun. With good-natured teasing, both parties take part and the teasing stops if someone gets uncomfortable. With verbal bullying, the bully keeps up the taunting even if the target asks him to stop. In fact, the taunting may get worse once the bully has upset his target.

A verbal bully might also spread rumors about her victim. She hopes that the rumors will keep others from being friends with the victim.

The Effects of Bullying

Bullying may seem like it is no big deal to a person on the outside. Bullying hurts, though. Imagine being afraid to go to school each day for fear that a bully will make fun of you in front of everyone.

Kids who are being bullied may start to spend more time alone. This can make depression and loneliness feel much worse, though.

The victims of bullying often feel helpless. They do not feel like there is anyone they can turn to to make the bullying stop.

Bullying has serious and lasting effects, even when the hurting is done using words. The victim likely feels **depressed**, angry, embarrassed, and scared. The victims of bullies often withdraw from their usual activities. They end up feeling very lonely. Even after the bullying stops, many of these feelings do not go away.

Who Gets Bullied?

Verbal bullies often look for targets who do not fit in in some way. The target may look different, wear clothing that is not like what others wear, or have a unique personality or interests. These kinds of traits give the bully something to focus her hurtful words on.

Studies have found that kids with disabilities are nearly three times more likely to be bullied than are kids who do not have disabilities.

Verbal bullies may target someone who is a loner because she does not have friends who will stand up for her.

Kids with disabilities, shy kids, or those who seem to have few friends are also common targets. The bully may feel he can pick on these types of people because no one will stand up for them. You can prove the bully wrong.

Why Do People Bully?

You might wonder why someone would want to hurt another person. Often bullies pick on others because they look down on other people. This means they do not feel like their target is worthy of **respect**. Everyone deserves respect, though.

Some kids are verbal bullies because their family members insult, threaten, and yell at each other at home. This is not an excuse for treating people poorly, though.

Bullies might pick on others because they think it makes them look more powerful or popular to their classmates.

Most bullies like the feeling of power they get when a target reacts to their taunts. Sometimes bullies pick on another person to make themselves feel better about something bad happening in their own lives. This is not an excuse for hurting other people. Bullying is wrong, no matter what the reasons behind it are.

Walking Away, Not Fighting

You might think that the best way to stop a bully is to fight him. Do not do this! Fighting could get you hurt. Fighting also lets the bully know that he is getting to you. This is exactly what a bully wants.

It is hard, but try to ignore the bully. If you can be **assertive**, make eye contact, and tell the bully firmly and calmly to leave you alone, you can try that. If you think you will sound angry or scared, just walk away.

The teachers at your school do not care who started a fight. They often punish everyone involved because fighting is dangerous and wrong.

Getting Help

One reason that bullying is so widespread and goes on for so long is that victims do not tell anyone about it. They may feel that telling someone will not help or that it might even make the bullying worse. This is not true, though.

Asking a trusted adult for advice is a good idea because she might have dealt with bullying as a kid herself. Even if she did not, she can still help you.

Talking to a friend about your feelings about being bullied is a good idea, too.

Telling a trusted adult, such as a parent, teacher, or coach, is important. Talking about how you are feeling will make you feel better. An adult can also give you advice on how to stop the bullying. She will know the right people to talk to if she cannot solve the problem with you on her own, too.

Improving Self-Esteem

Being verbally bullied can hurt a person's **self-esteem**. Self-esteem is a sense of self-worth. Do not let a bully's hurtful words take your self-esteem from you! Remember the bully does not know you as you know yourself and as your friends and your family know you. As harsh as the bully's words might be, they do not change who you are inside.

A counselor helps people talk about their feelings. He can give you advice about dealing with your feelings and rebuilding your self-esteem.

Volunteering to do something like helping out in a local park is an activity that can make you feel good about yourself.

If you are feeling sad, lonely, or depressed, talk to a parent, friend, or **counselor**. All these people can help you see the good things that they like about you. They can help you realize that being bullied is not your fault.

Bully-Free Schools

Many schools are trying to solve the bullying problem. Principals, teachers, and students in these schools work together to create bully-free zones. This means that everyone promises to watch for bullying and stand up for the victims. If **bystanders** become **witnesses** instead of standing by, the bully has less power to hurt others.

A lot of bullying takes place in hallways and stairwells. In schools with no-bullying policies, teachers and principals make sure these places are safe for everyone.

If your school is starting an antibullying program, teachers will talk to students about how to build a respectful community.

A bully-free zone does not happen overnight. Making one also takes work from the entire school community. Is your school ready to work together? You can talk to your principal or a teacher about starting a program to rid your school of bullying if it does not have one.

Taking a Stand

Next time you are sitting in your classroom, look at your classmates. You may be friends with some of these people. You may find that you have hardly spoken to other people in the room. It is okay not to like everyone, as long as you treat everyone with respect.

It takes strength to stand up to a bully. It also takes strength to see the good qualities in every person and to show everyone respect. Are you up to the challenge?

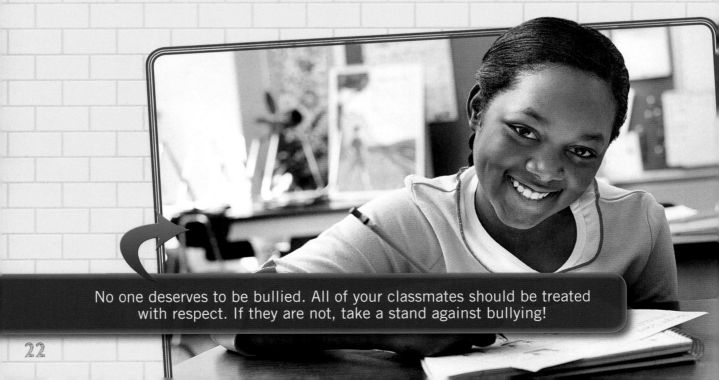

No one deserves to be bullied. All of your classmates should be treated with respect. If they are not, take a stand against bullying!

Glossary

assertive (uh-SER-tiv) Being firm in a positive way.

bystanders (BY-stan-derz) People who are there while something is taking place but are not part of what is happening.

counselor (KOWN-seh-ler) Someone who talks with people about their feelings and problems.

cyberbullies (SY-ber-bu-leez) People who do hurtful or threatening things to other people using the Internet.

depressed (dih-PRESD) Having a sickness in which a person is very sad for a long time.

exclude (eks-KLOOD) To keep or shut someone out.

humiliate (hyoo-MIH-lee-ayt) To make someone else feel very bad about himself or herself.

physical (FIH-zih-kul) Having to do with the body.

respect (rih-SPEKT) Thinking highly of someone or something.

self-esteem (self-uh-STEEM) Happiness with oneself.

verbal (VER-bul) Using words.

witnesses (WIT-nes-ez) People who see things happen and step in to stop people from being hurt.

Index

Websites

Due to the changing nature of Internet links, PowerKids Press has developed an online list of websites related to the subject of this book. This site is updated regularly. Please use this link to access the list:
www.powerkidslinks.com/subp/words/